praise for *an easy place / to die*

"Vincent Cellucci's poetry does not resemble anybody else's, and I don't mean by that just the poetry of his contemporaries. What he does with words is he makes them carry several kinds of speech in the most concise and musical manner. Among those kinds is a New Orleans jive known only to cooks and musicians, a fast talking rap with sharp glinting edges like a chef's knife. There are soft passages, too, moments of illuminated tenderness that make this word-landscape foggy sometimes, but never imprecise. The dude knows moves. Look for him in the big leagues."

Andrei Codrescu
Editor, *Exquisite Corpse*
Author, *Jealous Witness: New Poems*

"Vincent Cellucci is a poet who pries open the fissures within words and syntax to release evanescent meanings we barely register before they dissipate. But in that moment, we learn how much more our words could say—if we dared to let them."

John Biguenet
Robert Hunter Distinguished University Professor
Loyola University in New Orleans
Author, *Rising Water* **and** *Shotgun*

"In Vincent Cellucci's first collection the question of how to speak of something (a place, a time, a situation), is really the question of how to live with it, and oneself. Damage to damage, in unpredictable and compelling, jazz-influenced rhythms, "in the muddied eddies of other eyes," and broken across shard-like enjambments, the poet's reflections expose the uncertainty of our fragile (collective and competing) dreams of identity and community. *An Easy Place/ To Die* is an uneasy book, but its inclusiveness and the wrenching speed of association are a way of keeping the heart right there—while "assembling the semblances of survival" in new ways—to remind us that if sincerity is to matter it has to be carnal."

Laura Mullen
Poet and Professor
Louisiana State University
Author, *Murmur*

"Those who've lost charge with Mademoiselle Poesy will be thoroughly re-entranced by the songe of her inimitable smile here. M'sieur Cellucci is a masterful cantor. These poems are the ghost signatura Rx for an ancient metropolis dying before our eyes, La Nouvelle-Orléans to be sure: 'the bottom sunrise…and blood / suck mosquitos…pave your face…me gustaria muerta' Moreover, as providence would have it, Cellucci's lettres (and the pleasure is ours!) are in response to a telegram sent by the Bull of Heaven Herself. And just as the Ur-task of the poet is to scribe, Cellucci's reply is steadfast to that purpose; and wholly consigned as agent of the 'undesirable grail quest am i.'"

Dave Brinks
New Orleans Poet and Editor, *YAWP*
Author, *The Caveat Onus*

An Easy Place / To Die

An Easy Place / To Die

poems by

Vincent A. Cellucci

Baltimore, Maryland

© 2011, Vincent A. Cellucci

Library of Congress Control Number: 2010933430
ISBN: 978-1-936328-03-1

CityLit Project is a 501(c)(3) nonprofit organization
with offices in the School of Communications Design
at the University of Baltimore.
Federal Tax ID Number: 20-0639118

All rights reserved. No part of this book may be
reproduced or transmitted in any form or by any means,
electronic or mechanical, including photocopy, recording,
or any information storage and retrieval system,
without prior permission from the publisher
(except by reviewers who may quote brief passages).

Printed in the United States of America
First Edition

Cover and Book Design: Jonas Kyle-Sidell
and Vincent A. Cellucci
Book Design and Project Assistance:
Adam Romanofsky, Class of '11
Katie Baumer, Class of '10
Loyola University Maryland
Author Photograph: Jason Vowell and Wylie Whitesides
Cover Photographs: Dr. Gary King (foreground, thermophilic bacteria)
and Linzey Powers (background, City Park in New Orleans
after unusual snow, 2.12.10)

c/o CityLit Project
120 S. Curley Street
Baltimore, MD 21224
410.274.5691
www.CityLitProject.org
info@citylitproject.org

Nurturing the culture of literature.

Dedicated to the memories of Alfred, Amelia, and Philomena Cellucci and Jowena Conte

table of contents

I. Uruk—Cradlecasket

If said reader approaches said poem as a mountain lion	5
let	6
Partial *una*	7
BlueDelta	8
Bumbags at Washington Square's Gate	10
Kind Gardens, April 1957	11
Write Your Favorite Words	12
easy / sleeps	13
Partial *duae*	14
i've never seen him; I mean	15
Remnants	16
Ditchdigger	17
Insidiously	18

II. Ishtar Castles

Women Wishing Wells and Whitman	21
Nother	23
Suspect / To Your / Stomping / Grounds	24
Suspect / To Your / Stomping / Grounds 2	25
Upriver	26

Eyes / Bottle / You	27
Matter / For Mourning	28
keepnight / current	29
Armoire	30
If a river hollas in the woods	31
A Suffering / Breeze	32
finish lines	33
Moonbathing	34
Momentarily / Momentous	35

III. Death by Heaven's Bull

Partial *tria*	39
Me Gustaría / Muerta	40
I had a Room in New Orleans	41
White Azaleas / or Axioms for my Daughter	42
Grates	44
Port Work	45
How People Burn	47
Cleaning Up / Al's Apartment	48
Even heaven is blue	50
Auda*city*	51
Suprises / Lie	52

IV. ELIXIREXTINCTION

Mess / O / Pot / Amia	55
Before / Headstone	57
Shackled / Succulent	58
responsorial	59
Tell Me: / God Wasn't / Born Into Us	60
Causeway	61
exceptionalist manifesto + exceptionalist womanifesto	73
poet's prose	81
how's my dying? / please call	82
mise en place	83
about the poet	85
acknowledgments	86

An Easy Place / To Die

I. Uruk—cradlecasket

If said reader approaches said poem as a mountain lion

Instead of your bringing the Flood, let lions rise up and
  diminish the people.
                              Gilgamesh, *(XI, iv) Gardner*

                    temptation *gives*
slip back into soothing rituals or a pair of boots
(one of my best friends
                    staring at the crucifix again)
re-read that favorite novel   this time defying
                                        the protagonist
                                        is e*mpathy* hunting
younger now   promenade in the begonia garden that sits in nana's lap
than we'll ever be again   move back to your favorite waste land
                                        this time sans control
                                        replace: *create*
rediscover our orbits and train moons to retain
reclaim a lighter to re-align with Prometheus
the longer this line the Father I defy   gravity   inhale toxic fretless flight
   (worth skipping a breath or two)
half the fire requires we
smother light spans dark twins
ask the maenad why the skeletons bite epitasis   offends husbands
and never offers black dye

        suspect the expected

            let's not and say we died—
                            snow taming time

let

Helios begin again—
share the armrest

Loadada and Loadmama
make universe
dance whenever they get horizontal

sun cries witness
between kernels of popcorn
and swigs of sprites

bare parents
nature rear:

Mountain down my child
Moon up son
Act like a lake little lady

adolescent orbits speed
earth parents
no choice but to let—

inertia thrusts more
than all the world's pelvises

gravity attracts us like magnets
underworld

Partial

una

I'm not Christ
I don't think clearly

some days
I walk
in the rain I relate

trudging
through
the pack   passing sweat
laying on
alms
beads
drop on transparent hairs
ejected from the bicep
not resurrecting
posthumous hides
vestiges moribund

that chorus
        seized us
apostles   cannibals

earth lulls
longer than we hear

BlueDelta

Dedicated to Jamey Hatley

All forgotten grease
Crackles golden

Don't throw none   bother none
whoeva you looking for   idn't here
        come now   depends
        get on out my house

you know good and damn well my story's about to fire
                a warning bullet
                    piercing my heart
                          sealing my lips

Sure   was walking by
        on that gravel path
                back from the salvage yard
 stopped to wipe my brow
        with my shirt   and I see
Memphis Minnie pouring boy angels
                watering the magnolia outside
                wearing mother's dead face

Shoulda known
        them boys wouldn't grow
what's left   lasts too

set settled folks groaning
moons and stars amass   moonnstarsnstarsnmoons

        fighting like animals puffing up in their bellies
Every time
that grave parade
        passes
that barefoot boy   weighted in sweaty clothes
beats his drum
    hung
        like a dingy apron round his neck
                his trick   to take off

                        dead   up
                    not his face   up   up
                        magnolia limbs kept reaching

Right now I suspect
                anyone   with any sense
                                    or them same eyes
                        pleading for help
so many years ago
        dusk pinched her
                        kept her

Bumbags at Washington Square's Gate

To Shippy

There's a man next to me freezing
twirling a broken leaf by its stem

all the bums have duane reade needs
those bags best for the afterlife?

don't quote the shadow playing guitar
on this
    but the squirrels are getting closer

around us
sun photographs
the park's malaise

man with mustard shoes
mistakes me for a lighter

people like me   like him
            stop
   mid street   shiver
curse themselves
                   turn
back to loiter in strangers
my thoughts follow

another leaf on the ground
dead trees holding hands

Kind Gardens, April 1957

To Ruth Ann Robinson[1]

Spring is coming. Soon it will be here.
March 21 is the first day of Spring. Easter
comes in springs. We get new suits
for Easters and good hats too.

I like springs when the birds come. Don't they sings
pretty songs? The robins lay eggs. The eggs
are blues. Best of all
my birthday comes then.

I like springs because there are blues birds
on my feeders. They eat seeds. When Spotty
the dog comes out all the birds fly away.
Baseball teams come back too.

We have lots of flowers in our backyard. I asked
mother if I could have some for school. I wanted
a daffodil. So we took some dirt and put
it in a pot. Then we dug up the daffodils
and planted them. We put white paper
around the flower pot and took it to school.
We are going to watch it bloom. Water comes every day.

---

1 This poem utilizes verses from Room 202 of the Philadelphia Kindergarten (J. H. Brown) class my mother attended. Ruth Ann Robinson seemed an apt symbolic name of the American time period that gestated this work. Ruth Ann began the first stanza; my mother's stanza is the last.

Write Your Favorite Words

Write your favorite words
with yellow highlighters in the sun

Where to
constant chastenaut?

Capture your highness
remind her of the things she loved

Fall in love with isolation
abstain, bathe in murky tears
drip-prick-dry on holly
stain your nails with wild berries
wear a wardrobe of children woes
surf storm surges on a tortoise shell
home with the workers and bric a brac
your pillow   an Asian girl pens:

Cry when we ignore the fantastic

Stay silent   say yes
  then retreat

easy
sleeps

on the sheets
  he doesn't use enough

listenen to paul thibs
  play a twelve string

sings: *feels like im fighting*
            a war on my own

I swat a nightfly on my knee
last smell: cookie scented candle from my aunt

   door unlocks
                          by itself
   dire conversation
                    nativities self destruct

we are as close
to sober
as we allow
              the ring we been in for awhile now
                    Tomorrow   insufferable mist

                          we have all night for exchanging
                                last words
blossoms of gloom
blow from north to south

tonight
      we keep falling
                  how needs win

Partial

duae

Wonder if Christ had perfect
vision—misshaped
cornea of a King—
brambles in mine
could he too be blind?

we are closed precious
open for no precaution
friends   brothers
ricochet like bullets

I don't climb to crucifixion
but bless the cross
I'm restrained to

our fingers felt for wind and friends
in the dark
outcast dens of the flooded
and destitute
              wells

even today
we have the same delusions
internalized beneath
cracked skin and rashes

we minded the scars
rope same and sandals

won't comb our hair
or examine halos
in mirror water

i've never seen him; I mean

i am the absolute
          abhorrence
i consecrate your enormous role

dead bog man
guards garbage
scrubs his furnace
with baby's breath?
we god's droppings—

surgeon failed
found a little girl's shoe
on the side of the road
merciless dreamboat

remember when smooth
caprice succeeded
could be made anew

our missed belt loop
prick in the thicket
cold wooden floors
no reason for tonight

shining the shores
you love to long for
that lie about yourself
you can't tell anymore

the bottom sunrise
of fingernails and death-white paper

Remnants

For Brock Guthrie

two green bell peppers
spoil in a stolen grate
outside Sav-A-Center
     sweat-stained
  megalomaniacs line to Tip's
for vampire music
     & blood
    suck mosquitos
a domicile
turned   sacristy
febreezed
   smellnomurder
comingoutfromin
    that's welfare   that's wild
that's we how love sounds
         my friends
forbid beers to get warm
smoke like they're
in the trenches

toilet's duct taped
urinal mortared with several bags
of ice
   big tits, short hairdo enters
the restroom same time as I zip my fly
my antagonist sits pisses
with door unlocked exits
after wiping back to front
says: *honestly* *you're writing*
in public yes indeed
  I'm the dirty
    summer blood
        boiling
        OVER

Ditchdigger

"What do you do?"

The ditchdigger eclipses grave
            corpse, and sun
his arms, tied to the shovel

When it rains
        the potent reminder
   he digs his own
   by the numbers   centimeters, a plot
      of mud   clumps the bottom of his boots
tonight
     in this storm the depth line reaches his calf
    where the big muscle bows to bone
   right there
   the position
  ground's
 gifts he unwraps
or how deep he's fallen
     into his vocation
          his palms coffin more than calluses
  his toes embalm their tread on wet skin soles
before the flowers and tombstone there are some weeds
                      maybe grass
  Once in awhile   flowers
the dark wind
beguiles again

Insidiously

Insides have problems
insides have reams
of disappointed dreams
remembered inside
eyelids inside upturned
sun-visors insidious
half inside smelling
half inside tasting
our insides spoiling
inside inside's offspring
I wish inside no words
bottle no sand inside hour
glasses don't read inside
don't see inside
secretly hates peace
a roman raping rituals
inside the rectory
words hate inside
inside breathes beam
radiate inside's anatomy
throbbing insides wonder
how long inside I have
before inside kills me

II. Ishtar Castles

Women Wishing Wells and Whitman

Women at the bar wishing wells
the vagrants have coins the drunkards
spend theirs on wells ¤ Penises purse pennies
roll and sack of semen spent like change
so many wishes never come
at last call comfort crawls to white azaleas
bed stains trailed towards mattressing snores
it's easy to abhor mortared cylindrical depth
especially when a boy with no illumination
discovers the blurred basement of his creation
(might have lost him to the cavern)
I motion to those heaping buckets of water
cause of pulley's design and elaboration
of leverage saturates the sustenance hydrates
highlights the mission of procreation ¤ I think
Whitman had it right when he wrote: no more
heaven nor anymore *hell than there is right now*
urge and urge and urge
always the procreant urge of the world
Whitman urges this poem forward
I share the boy's allure of copper
or nickel ¤ The fulfillment of desire
the completion and security of the first sip
of water out of the first city well
a desire forced by necessity
instead of whim ¤ The precious success
when the wish submits and returns
by the bucket load an unrequited take
contaminates the well and the population
desires the rope and knot make it a double
knot or triple or quadruple tied tight
the night is the land settled on our city
nothing moves without first weaving
I've written nothing nice nothing
new just one true well
established position a young boy crowds
the circumference of a well
wishing he could multiply his body
like paper figure fences the girls cut
in school and surround his source

each fist clenched each fist clutches
the image of a man on metal
the treasure a currency
he will sacrifice his own
father or brother to abandon
in order to hear the plop
as metal breaks the water
he imagines the coin's spins
displace the water settles
amongst familiar busts
that never reveal
heads or tails ¤ If we do
anything we wish well

Nother

Sutra, it takes a map or a foreclosure
whole nother story   whole nother world
all nother's beginnings come
when nother has no one left to call
nother brother   nother lover   sappy pitch sadly
don't need nother   nother needs me   if nother
never ask you nother know glorious
strangers projected in newspaper profile stench
apple mention junk haven
decades of stalling an exhumed term
the bear in nother's lighter mauled nother—
a cnn survivor   ribbon undone   nother owes an apology   settle
over a picnic of cheese and fucking in washington square?
nother will draw curtains around us and no one will see
each nother in our foils again   open them
the park   a stage still thrusting nother   always
inside of nother   but the crowd waits   puzzled
over the fact that nother's clothed in flannel   the fact
nother didn't orgasm provides some verisimilitude—
the change the bourbon wrecked guitarist throws
in nother's open case on the subway   if actions are character
know nother than fitzgerald   nother's fingers typing
this manuscript fix all the fuck ups of nother's history
in love and sham—the queen's garden   nother's sorry
nother's sad and lonely   nother in the moon is too
and oh how nother looks up to nother romantically like nother
nother turns nother on more than art   more than nother
good thing nother spent bucks on a thicker mattress pad
and pills hatch in nother's stomach
so nother's children don't hatch in nother's crimson canal

**Suspect
To Your
Stomping
Grounds**

     The last night I liked you
                         you withdrew
         not like from a bank   or snatching up a crap bet
         not like   but
                 exactly how you did—
aiming
away
sparing
       self pleasure   repelled
                            by my cocoa labia
you knew
       lying there   back surrounded   beneath
                              my stencil
     by dawn
     morning brings
           months of missing work and eating
     life roaming
          salvage yards for
              repair
              fingers
            such things— unlike me
                    who knows life masturbates
  more than me
       classic craft folds
                      skin
appalachian rounded skin   a hair or freckle   a wick
to light
     your limbs   pull away
                        as if you
                        were time himself   and we
were extinguishing
       ourselves from history

**Suspect
To Your
Stomping
Grounds 2**

                          Some lovers
                          model
wishes on forever   pose
                        for never's portrait
                                   nude   chill in the room   our duo
                                                                                 not allowed
in the same position til
timer runs out of sand
                                  with the same inertia
   he yanks away   we feather out

      call me ace   he say
hey   *I know*   *your favorite perfume*

                                     Her name Cherie
strange little whore name   strange little whore way of spelling it too
    don't pretend
                  I want to conquer you   speaking
of which   start pretending
you haven't   smothered me   when you
                  withdrew   I could barely breathe

Upriver

To Fos

Nother got brains, a library card, and an ibook
        but no place instructs   more than
              where nother refused to look
I've arrived
Mississippi—

Love's been
      someone else's
        Mississippi eyes
I've been amiss lately
            living my neighbors' lives
so that one day
    I have no life
        upriver
              it may snow bodies upon us

Where we go   going   we pretend
Life's always
    a carnival forgiving tomorrow
inside nother's insides inside of others

Fucking's a mess lately
        in the muddied eddies of other eyes

**Eyes
Bottle
You**

collected the eyes of every fish you ever speared
        fancied finger licking women
        done made a habit out of where you live
sit on them eyeballs
shit them
        stored in empty wine bottles
        on the rack next to where the best rest
have to humiliate me right
  wish to high heaven you do again
        be nobody to butt heads with after that
  nothing's sweeter than wheat dying in the sun

swinging elbows for cash and checks
soliciting sex with cheese
        broke wrenched you
        supper's in the sand
pretending swamps behind my ears
sassy as a jaybird
bulge with restless words
stole from mama's lower lip

the first fire—every time you get ashore
    clothesline strings salt out the wind
hoped in vain
could preserve time
rinse your skin
don't count the bottles
        or the eyes in those bottles

  at your funeral, package you in eyes
  everything you ever took casts you off

Matter
For Mourning

The best friend a person has is one who has just died.
                                            Marquez

Listening
      at the door between my neighbor's crying
                easily mistaken
                for laughter
            maybe coughing
              or fucking
everything's so awful   she screams to no one
                        me
                she just got the call
        and now calling back
          to Jesus no
          nor the deceased
          not even just to call
Feeling
      the forbidden urge to barge in
        and mother her – father her
          then love her
          because her
                  recent matter
                  for mourning
      assures no other life
               but one
  Telling
  instead
  I am paralyzed
    loving the fact of someone else

**keepnight
current**

dispel
      altogether now

I conduct through nother

      spectral explosions
always out renovating
plots nothers drop
from cradlecasket castles
constructed by slaves
and bridled beasts
over quicksand

intoxication   nother's moat
    & drawbridge

never promised
      nother wouldn't get drunk
off honey in the moon
lovemaking never
dependent
on running water
or electricity

nother's alone
even amongst friends

sink nother
swallow the flour of night
nother conducts through me
earth cakes nother's full mouth
consumes hope
heaven up there's more
castles on quicksand

Armoire

nother's moat
      of secrets
stuffed in
              back pockets
or pilgrimages averted
attention thrown
              to extinction?
nother's been deceased
              as many times
as nother changes
nother's clothes
or nother refills
nother's cocktail
              nother decides
   trucker hat & aviator glasses
              decide nother
   scotch on the rocks
      complimentary
         to courage & curiosity
nother's audible outsides
surprised   nother possesses
nother plays—
      nother reached
             & nother responded
wrong—

If a river hollas in the woods

        Glad I wolf
     Up am I
         I like nothers texture / can I text hers?
                       nothers gonna get a fuck nothers don't deserve
                 nothers where yas not
             topple top of
       Lick creek riverist
       I want nothers to say one more
once more
@ some point
        I'm going to have to tell nothers
        I love hers before shes tell me to go to hell

  exnothers explosions extinction   these are things
                                  nothers promises—
     nothers don't have to leave before nothers go
     nothers naked?
   when nothers get back / eat nothers leftovers
                   only distinction—the difference between
               obtainable and attainable   nothers in between
   Fairydevil bedfall
  sweetie nothers forgot
     nothers have to halve me
when nothers have me
           nothers heat
               sleeves the succulent sheathes as heel sounds sway
   lov*ing* (not love) succeeds   (even if it's the last sentence nothers read
                 cycloptic before sleep)

A Suffering Breeze

wanted to carpet you
or pave your face
as a driveway

you have the minutia of millions
not knows or cares
no pit or speck

when was the last time
I saw you last
Tallahasee or Galveston?

dumping your bait off a pier
or filling up your tank?

some of the things you lost
I might have (lost)

your sister said you were mean
meaning you hit
hookers like home runs

didn't do yourself any favors
did me a few
that did me in

finish lines

                        you blasted bombero
licking strawberry jam off a machete
straining mermaid juz
      from your mustache
plucking hairs over your
heart to the tune of: " I Care /
Fuck You" or "You Lose /
I Lose" is it coincidence
      that sun is sol
        or shit out of luck—
if not finished
      starved by a tremendous vulgarity
                  a festooned firebrand
                  a not night shiver

Moonbathing

sun burned sky
                for tonight
moon lit sky
                for us
  recline spines
        pianos
horizontal harmonizing horizons
    our lips umbrellas
lowered
       for each monsoon
Memory strikes
             two moons
in earth's sky—two reflected sun
   here   once was one

**Momentarily
Momentous**

let's try each other on for size
dressing room shall be the bedroom
anticipate insides
your race your wrapping paper
your bow your thong
destroy bed linens faster than
the child rips a carefully wrapped gift
i gift poems & my body & request
return
the world lies
lie with me
invent constellations
between our imperfections
trace with tongues
leave the lights on
because the only shit that might be significant
        this past second—
                      now gone

III. Death by Heaven's Bull

Partial

tria

We composed that other garden
you have forsaken
my god: our interrogation

when we stormed
not our rib caves we swaddle
    deflected heaven and earth
    organs host

we enjoy the brackish taste
of tears toppled

we take the slow boat
to scales
we devour

we both died
no matter

    we are some partial
  spirit

shadows
shorter than
our next footstep
ruined earth

Me Gustaría Muerta

        contact   nothing
                        can be
    said   can't can do
    nothing   acts on
        contact
              evinces us we have
        minds
takes all
                saturn-ringed deceivers
   christen me in contact
   forgo nothing   jumping
       over something for everything
            spies
            someone dies
                    or someone dead
even before
    the punishment
              muerta—
the reaper's favorite effable appearance:
                    me gustaría
                    muerta

this procession says:
      breathing
         confesses
              wanting

I had a Room in New Orleans

Four years the fan never stopped spinning
the walls painted in buoyant blood
and the curtains fogged in light
we slept on a mattress on the floor
next to the chess board and the bong
on my bedside table. An inherited
oriental rug incubated the wooden floor
my bedroom compact with only one outlet
the floor swathed in extension chords
every time I tripped, I fell asleep
sometimes the walk-in closet swallowed us
me, em, and my bed, all krill
in the porpoise's esophagus. He inhaled
us up his nasal passages, met his mammoth brain
a lofty billow directly above, the mattress
lifted up, ejected over his blowhole and above
the fan we sauntered like aerosol mists
marooned in the dim golden room
Sometimes, I'd wake in a vomit pool I spread
and slapped up on the wall when I was drowning
in my own 6 ft. swells—the last finger of a sinker

White Azaleas
or Axioms for my Daughter

Life's those glass snow globes, fragile but must be turned upside down and shaken before you see the beauty.

A human is a fleshfish.

People possess their notions of God; don't allow them to possess yours.

Remember to remember.

Some people collect stamps or coins; collect love.

Skin is the soul's jewelry.

Drugs are fire hydrants; they can save you when you need them but park in front of one or leave one running and you'll get towed or extinguished.

We are doodles to death.

Easy to fall in love with people you don't know, but loving the ones you do makes matter.

Don't you don't.

Could wind be a wish on us?

Let's leave to a song.

Use imagination, not others.

Once you're shattered, you're together.

You are what you read.

You have antennas; don't neglect them.

Keep one head in the books
    other one on the ground.

Better to err on the side of reckless.

Extinction is the Earth's shower after the haircut of the human race.

This world is also
    an easy place
        to appear.

Grates

sis and i's
rooms were drained
by grates
mine was clogged
(blind patch) seepless
in our symmetry
i peered
down my sister's grate
most nights while she slept
both relieved to be washed
down as if funneled to a secret
portal kim dreamed   i spent
nights rotating in her whirlpool

i saw adam work
and eve march
powered into copulation   the grate
serrated my soulshop saw-
ing my parents' resignation
to each other   spraying dust
and debris up through the grate's wide
screen   hacked in half
they separate on the floor

scenes piercing through grates
required goggles but i had no
safer quarters   my fingers coiled
inside the black metal frame
2 eyes and 2 ears barreled
down (caged in) the ceiling

Port Work

the dead file soul to soul
buffet of living imagination
coffin pine   sanded smooth
in the mill of dreamwork
hyperamnesia history's hindsight
Christ considers this port closed

Regardless, enter kitchen's
rising tides   no wake zone

ripples of not finishing dinner on time
chair, a slide and table, a brigade
of a hundred peas marching in paces
around catsup sea and mustard mountain
dehydrated, crossing sands sara lee
to a tundra of undressed salad
        bulging cartography
           shrug and play on the plated terrain
inedible, the oven timer fetches
    6:56 PM
4 minutes
        to finish
  a digital tombstone
a drunk chase upstairs
       the belt cracking
         melting polar ice caps
             crash
                    down sea stairs

submarines descend into ceiling
rising tides require
           raising the grate-scope
people love some torture
water logging, pruned fingers of an houred bather
                      your hands are frequencies
       before you die
sinusoidal waves needles
  reading the lies of your life
polygraphic fingers point below

                        the descent
                        diver bellows:
    im so simple death
          i spoil like a banana left in sun
                    the adult cocoon
                        vestigial too
the stance:
body as pendulum
clouds and reflection knees
skull bows feet
worship a right angle
                        jack knife
                        last action
            no splash

How People Burn

To one of my closest few

First he failed his brother's heed
after his elder tackled him twice!
(my advice) off bikes, the slam

shook the shotgun's frame
the sound was superseded deafened
by the violent pedals & silent score

the chain squeaked as he sped
back again with gasoline; promised
what he was craving

Torch the nigger torturer
of my dreams—such words
last words from fixless lips

It was a Tuesday, 10PM
a MidCity block ignited
twice a pair of headlights passed

We, who only dabbled with
Vengeance rocked on the porch confiding—
death over Angola condemned

how we were the headlights
& our words burn between brothers
flames too rich to reach

Cleaning Up
Al's Apartment

the hurricane: mental illness
perpends the soul's spinnaker

we walking graveyards. inside, we all hold the dead. clean them alive.

"going to be bad"
"worse than you think"

sitting on cracks in the concrete watching the jersey ants stipple
my legs before squishing them. my uncle and father eating plastic wrapped
wa wa fruit & hard boiled eggs. I fast.

inside:

recliners with urine and shit stains which we sat on
towels used once, dampened, too dirty to use again
thus piled with the trash on the floor or in the tub
in which he couldn't possibly shower
a bed never slept in
a tv it took two months to plug in
scribbles, notes, attempt-to-do-lists still satiate independence
condoms in the dresser, just in case, next to clothes, new
debris: sprayed bars of scrubbed soap
black path across the pattern walked floor

after peeling two month's paper towels, opened soup cans, plastic cups,
and liters of root beer off the floor with an impromptu shovel,
a small one handled pot—the smell
of ammonia

replaced what I thought would be the strongest smell in my memory.

I had a mask when I picked Hiram's possessions out of moldy Marengo.

we haul 2 dozen bags of filth to the dumpster
like nawlins: too much trash to filter—it all goes
the coroners (the national guard) even picked up some
just enough for us to return and clean ourselves

the bathroom we refuse to go into until last; dad scrubs sink, toilet, tile—
purification regrets: I moved.

pass on some matter to Camden—passed Whitman's grave *to disengage myself
from those corpses of me, which I turn and look at where I cast them*

maybe because dad scrubs and cleaned what I left
maybe because there's just one filthy floor
instead of a city
maybe because soap's the mold, sickness the sludge

smiles sting our why faces why our jokes alive
treading in each others' sweat in summer's cities amongst swards
of a life
lives
cleaned up
in a day
never

Thermophiles sharing
our all mess

prepared me for these
immaculate introjections

taking, the process of reclamation. humans in waste lasting.
assembling the semblances of survival.

Even heaven is blue

Dedicated to Desha Beamer

since world disposed of you
pitcher of sun sweet tea
minnows raised us right
don't know how I've given up
how I hold a door open
like a gentlegun
like salt on fried
surprise   you're not—
ain't me a razor
to slice the only thing
that resides in me
your memory's steep
whirlwind in a cemetery
one chance for infinity
you buried mountains
bury you

Audacity

Initially went to sleep bearing our own cries. Bleared hallucinations gore sleep— nightmare's sunnyside up. Bear now hangovers as the Sewage and Water Board pump the funk of New Orleans into a Bull. All slow process. Soon, those winged turn out right overhead. Bear mind. Fireport doldrum fathoms. Regardless, a fallen oak grates the top of a Dodge off Esplanade. Deserted neutral ground. A putty knife, new panes, and scrape escapes. Common as curb thousand fridge duct taped. In all this filth, cherish a primitive embrace. Roof of the Family Discount Liquor Store. A stray and you. Make eye contact. Both stare the Guard's Hummer down. Armed strangers have redeeming qualities. We both bang our heads into our walls. Prefer to hydroplane our own hearse. Bear.

Surprises
Lie

A thief has stolen my flesh.
Death lives in the house where my bed is,
and wherever I set my feet there Death is
          Gilgamesh, *(XI, v) Gardner*

stretched to opposition
      BLOATED ex lovers
  found dead
    underneath covers of crystal
         filaments
    remind
    how many the heavens murder

    angel's sip
    the bounty

if hell
  you burn
     eternally
heaven
  you drown
     fortunately   in firmament's
           greatest waters

IV. ELIXIREXTINCTION

Mess
O
Pot
Amia

To Ashlee

red exit signs
sexydistrict
scratching hairs
black TVs big screens foiled
on curbs—denim mud puddles
quarters jingling   bar flashlight
so much time corresponds
to nothing
coolers of fruit fermenting
hold the line
hold your toe
hip hop around with your middle
fingers partying
telling the police screaming
heaven is *hell*
pocket prison—
I searched the backseat
for illegal contraband
finding nothing
that's right motherfucker!

afterlife is not *dramaticrecovery*
the lovely the lost the least
Thermophiles
packed in the Quarter
past Decatur & let me
show you my new Car—
                    ondelet
pronounce
the French—*you're wrong*
socks off
        accurate
                desensitization
only sequins and feathers
        but Lawd the darkness

feels so good underneath
your underwear feels so smooth
like one dark corner
underneath the stairs

Before
Headstone

      sure of the wide world
          I sleep extinct sleep

first fear of the dark
      comforts Now
        —absence like sun—
traded glasses for welder's mask
earth organ emits a symphony of four-legged heads
          specifications for life form next
                lurking strangers
        freezing seas
        melting mountains
tomb or no tombs
      pyres or sky burials
            ground or mound

dead neverreally

final jazzy fact: extinction
          trapdoor of life

      make sure there's a sousaphone
      on the last-line
          no one will never exist—
   Alas   understated
    nobody beat body
          this battlefield separated
by pillows
   we barely born

Shackled
Succulent

                         Smart to
leave   your body   split
this
    suffering breeze

thunder
circles
    a bleached pebble path
some soldier's solace

                      No strength ain't noble
we jubilate we praise we syncopate we devastate
our futures
        shackled
        succulent   we
fire menagerie exploded corpses
   the more you next to me
   the more we perennial

responsorial

just dwindle
into oblivion
lonely right now

cassock of caskets
no casus belli

stegosaurus' dwellings
blues fast

down down and alone

¡feliz extinction!
smiles the fire

one
extinction at a time

**Tell Me:
God Wasn't
Born Into Us**

              fuck the white house
    I'm taking over
heaven

poor boy
        got killed
              purchasing a po boy
course it was over drugs
or a hundred dollars
most folks never
        draw
          the blinds
up over their own insides
raised knowing nothing
belongs to us in this world
usurping yourself come true

I once was
        gracious in
      an easy place
          to die

never again is enough said
next life: survive

Causeway

> *More important than having*
> *been born is your city*
> *the scale upon which your*
> *heart when you die will*
> *be weighed*
>   Alice Notley

      iff

          there no more penicillin
"you don't believe that yourself"

              more
              i dream
              solely
              of acetylene

"is that uncomfortable?"
"world's uncomfortable"

          showing me the handsome
          role of the ridiculous—
   fear gurgles self satisfaction:
       our den: separation
place-setting
      who else missing?

   she stumble wish-strong   crosslegged
          on a moldy rug
              unswept oblivion
              illicit liberties
waiting to be severed
from despair

        ∝

    Find us
    throw our corpses in jail

       Ancient stamens
       ice around pools
white flames wonder
      how i love Americans
      who (haven't) waited
      on the corner to grab canned water and MREs

         ∝

Next sterling'll find another
ruin before night is through

      in the Cabildo, Andrei told a room full

    somehow
       what's important to me always is said

      against: grind my time compete bare

  wanted to experience our big event
  people ask gods for such things
      gods give   bridge blessings collapse—
                been blessed enough
                be blessed again

         ∝

Amass the lovely the lost the least
     Thermophiles
packed the Quarter
past grandmother Decatur's long hair
      reminds us of a neglected time machine

     boiled leather to flat screens
     show you our new car

        "Baby, I don't have any clothes"
        "It's okay, I don't have a stomach"

∞

    Sacraments rejoice
magic compiles
           dying ships
                        cypress mangroves
                        seep august

                Flammablexperiencentimental
          adlibbing
                our pier on fire

        i can't taste without

∞

    Nola
caresses her freshly amputated breast

∞

              2-year-olds'
              penniless laughter

        world not my oak tree
        world not my umbrella
                    nor circling the creaking mile
                    tow truck that tows a tow truck

diving not even
in the sludge—which
an indelible task I saw
        still smoldering precipitation

        Andrei said
        crucial
        to remember New Orleans
        originated in tragedy
        Katrina, the latest
                sapping

∞

      leave please
Anyways our home
don't long entanglement
      the dud ultimatums   taste like old tomatoes
          exploded
           when handled
                    brackish, vaporized
                    remains
                              trial and burial
                              several disappearing skins
        draped the Tree of Life's limbs
        letter tacked to trunk reads:

        dear America,
            Love,
                        who
                  you   know

            i write your name in disbelief.

                ∝

Again moisture decks moss
marked texts opened outside

                streetcar line collide sounds up
                up ahead again

pencil sketch resolution yet to vote not on:
        south in snowflakes
            deliver flavored mud and moon

                ∝

tub threats
showered in sediment
fed poison off cobblestones too old
        the ghosts
            step one two feet closer to robbing them pennies

∞

don't moi want numb
we year old
        corrupt our colonies ditch morsels
        our fallacy
        by the throat
                waning's on sale

mention: design flurries
        down down and alone
        white battlements blot extinction

                2 horses faster than 1

∞

                No fingers tiny hair or smiles...
                New Orleans for months—
        Remouthing Brinks bringing Mina back
        walking around the Quarter   adults in awe

waste land: undesirable grail quest am i
        several snowflakes sighted in New Orleans this afternoon

∞

            we
        swarm to crypts
                crease
                hinged between raindrops   smooth
                      black fissures—doldrums in
                our mind's
        uprooted pentagrams rescuing corpses
song again makes tears come ubiquitous, memorized
                        volunteered
            my insides don't require CPR
                    nor before I knew eternity
            vines & spiders listened
    as phantoms purchased
        prostitutes *salilus*

∝

        Cher thrones a stool
        a fleur-de-lis necklace
        strangling   we all
        are entangled
        by the same   ornament
        its six tentacles   raised

∝

Who has *brought this one here*

∝

           Peggy's
           end to shore
           six parade ransom
      budweiser strings the bathroom
to be a sturgeon
marching the streets
acoustic opened *this hard*
bawling into *the start*
scientists sing:
      no one said it
      no one ever said
      take me back

∞

        Mess
        O
        Pot
        Amia

```
open mud huts
grooming hairs
scratching bites
broken tools              packed
on dirt paths
animals curt wail         when I say
so much time corresponds    it
to nothing                suitcase          nagbu
mortars of fruit fermenting  wish it was you  lured like the doe
                                              savoring a deer lick
```

∞

    Today smashed crickets of shame
    not when when was happening
    nor wind destroying
        nor when when was finally fucking mending
    (minutia of millions) don't hear yourself believe

```
old crickets
forgotten     bc it doesn't snow here
              why I say it does
cities'
emergency: no phantastikon
inept spells of our own
titled: delight
```

    lightening bolt pilot eyes of daystorms

∞

        fire of friends
        lapses into friendly fire
    i save
    u talk

                        repeat
                        fiery geode facts: gators don't sweat

                                        ∝

                                                Arallu. . . more
                                                flaming inscription men
            these roots break through
                        concrete
                                bioluminescent crepe myrtle coal offerings:
                                                                Nolus
                                                        awaits
                                                                        another
                                                        easy place
                                                        to appear

                                        ∝

        Humidity of breath air
                two storms collide
            moist monsters speak
            of graduated attrition
        all conversations at Molly's or Mae's
        bar cries open mirrors—
                        not even the FBI
                        drawing up on me   or OPP

                                        ∝

                        still fish
                        still drink
                        still screw
                                        found myself tasted the same

                                        ∝

                Surrender cheers
        uphold killess
                        control
        shot armpits
                        assault rifle strap on shoulder
                                another horizon   our arc

                                        waits to be dumped
                                        in a mass grave
            "is that uncomfortable?"
            "world's uncomfortable"
                        and today smashed   her last steps
                                        scum of entrails
                                            "you really moving?"
                    —barer than blurry

                                ∝

            moose moves morosely
            around his brother's carcass
            nothing sadder than a dead brother

                            hunter's presence removes him not
                            & if the stalker only knew
                            he'd be terrified

                                ∝

Westward grief sets
waiting to be stolen
majestic free like ferns
blooming outside
Sav-A-Center
                        am i undesirable?
                finally second best
                local superstition shares me
                                shame
                                -peat
                                    garbage rotting
                                                our
                                            maggot feather
                                            offerings encapsulate
                    underneath nation's hills sweat sin—
                                    we worthless dwellings

                fire the last drop
                        muy enferma of extinction

∝

    Believe the aforementioned
    this life's remission
             napkin comes to that
             evidence worthless receipts
                  crickets of shame
                      caresses conjure Atlantis
             reflections
             somehow *pure*—

∝

    that cricket never finishes Nother *said*
    when Insides *are cursed it was almost Louisiana*

∝

young flames mount the pyre

∝

    8-29-05
      06
      07
      08 (Gustav)
      09
      10 (BP Oil Leak in Gulf)

∝

Brinks cured & spoke later
Imagine a City with no Children
not a single Child   cried played
walked below hunched adults
didn't hold her hand

∝

    just poured the perfect beer
        for you Gilgamesh & trembled
    like you did years ago

> our blood was lighter fluid
> and we were sent
>   to the furnace
> bearing our friends
>   a sonnet of immolation:

Hiram, Aunt Jo, Pat, Chuck, Sarah, Emily, G, Peyton, Desha, Sarah B., Hanley, Saige, Erin, Marco, the Foul Train: Munney, Walker, Alex, Brian, Hayne (got off the Train), Wylie, Nicole, Pa, Cooper, Towbin, Egg Nog, Louisa, Mumpsie, Dan, Mike, Blake, Dedi, StevO, Anna Banana, Walshy, Mike V, Constantine, Jeff & J Lop, Bruno's Leslie, Miss Leslie (rip), Kingpin Mike, Tony "don't be saying my name bro", our Tulane girls: Louisa, Erin, Carey, Tanya, Lauren, Kim, Katies K, R, & B, Krissy, Whit, Fabien, Mae's Al, Squirrel, Darren, Duffy, Ian, Rebecca, David, Eric, Moonlight Chris, Dan Hershey, Greg Gz, Jeanne, Marc, Bob, Thibs, Bros: John, Paul, Sienna, Bill, Dillon, Walt, Erock, Juicebox, J, Mikey, jMCt, Stacey, J1, J2, Chef Drew, Remy, Bart Bell, Snake Bite, Beaker, Military Dave, Big D, Clem, Steph, Hunt, Portland Jeremy, Lance, High-T, Mama V, Kelly (rip), Kermit, Crazy Dave, Tedly, Ronnie Roo, Swaino, even Big Al, Red Mike, San Antonio Joe, Cole, Katie Belize, Liz, Big-Tittied Amber (sorry), Emily C., Meg, Gracie, Ben Low, Fez, Yoda, Ben, Red Dragon, W, Jammer, Theo, Shera, Greg, Rebo, Mary, Ashlee, Critta, Brugh, Scotty-doesn't- know, Kurt, Sammy, Tom Leg, Sadie, Malena, Fuego, Jonesy, McCay, Parker, Sunday, Andrei, Laura, Strip Club Mike, Alton, Cdiddy, BrookeBrock Mtn., Brinks, Jason V, Marsha, Derrick&Caroline and Pete&Jenny

∝

bull shark obsession swims upriver
                            PREDATORsalinetopristine
sirloined our Sordid-Offering

∝

Sati sequins on Audubon's grass
incorporating
words fresh kudzu electricity for a sec
snow makes sense
3 moonlit summers
assure the exhausting
breath of the Mississippi
will not extinguish—
                distant extant:

            a nother
            appears
    "Hey   Come here"
        "I am here"

exceptionalist manifesto

+

exceptionalist womanifesto

Exceptionalist Manifesto

Exceptionalism is
         my proudest embarrassment

                          collects exploding
                          fuses confused
         colludes seclusion excludes communion

demoralizes dignity dine starved
         cacti underwater
         willows hysterical
         meditates whims horrendous home billows

Exceptionalist sole etymology, the
                  blind seer
                  (simple extravagance)

      Exceptionalists immortal

no Exceptional warranties:
we
    forge receipts
    plow wilderness
    unpluck fruit
                    quiet commotion
                    anchor buoyancy

immediate artifacts
         don't belong to Exceptionalism
                          or its tenements:
                              completely inadequate
                          except in radical compliance
                    caress contemplate careless
Exceptionalists, ugly whore goddesses

         we confine omnipresence
         we fuck paralyzed and dance dive

Exceptionalists don't eat
         to survive; we eat

                                          to surrender domineer
                    teeth white flag scepters

Exceptionalists hungry
because they satisfied
passed out
on platters

can't wait to meet an Exceptionalist
can't wait to buy a souvenir at the landfill

                            everyone's exceptionally sane right now
                                                          they're not

                            everyone wishes Exceptionalism never existed
                                  saying such saves

nonsense out mouth and everything else on paper, such is Exceptionalism

everyone's just
Exceptionalists without
                                    redemption of a death raft
                                    or mini mountain
                                    on scale of telegrams
an illiterate read the Exceptionalist genesis
mocks Exceptionalism sincerely

Exceptionalism's iconography: a tow truck towing a tow truck
                                or a fire department afire
                                (tailoring a spit suit)

no rules nor women left dying fecund phallus racists castrated
                                                                      represent resent
fathers playing catch with their bastards

it's the fallaciousest fact

Exceptionalism: river well
                          never nigger say   I fucking hate everyone that loves
                                                        Exceptionalism or me

                    Except Exceptionalism
                    Accept Exceptionalism

already owns you
                    next year of your next life we find you
                    will murder our prodigious disaster

I'm not fucking kidding about this Exceptionalist shit

                    they pull their eyelashes out to construct bridges

you, Science, and I have
                    determined Exceptionalism

                                  a trinity absence like sun
                                  in iridescent mud missed

    come now impotence
                climax along
Exceptionalists suffer from euphoria
                        sacrifices wincing wolves to rabid sheep
criminal servants: classic Exceptionalist
                    mix extremes
          amen's amendable…

family is exceptional but I never confer with Exceptionalists

                    addicted to instability
                        procreate extinction

       we purest cancer

misplaced disclaimer: The Exceptionalist Manifesto contains 100%
misinformation amiss as to what an Exceptionalist or Exceptionalism is

not one Exceptionalist   exists
                            as an Exceptionalist
                                    resist

                        thankstaking
                        thousand second thoughts
                                thwart

Exceptionalist Womanifesto

    Nothing drums
                Exceptionalism

            like   suppressing it
              silence shouts
              stone breathes
                  owns the sun
              settles eternity: the dust
                            spins an exception
  our faithless refine
          salute
              corpses blocking keyholes
                        seven times
mine
          superinfancy
                anger's angels
                      pull hair—
  finger heaven
          p.s. infinity
          plugged with puddles

sky roots gnaw the bonds off Exceptional nourish—

how thou shalt not presume
            explain or concede

rain roof always
fire freezes
ice seethes
disdain opensclose   credits
              of man's punyverse
            a snap's reign—
Tomorrow: Tinyguy, I founded
          therefore I eat
                              Exceptionalists chew
                              morsel of metamorphosis
         lick lips
day after   nay night before
              work works
              play plays

                        chaos arranges
                        spittle exchanges   Exceptionalists don't pay our do's
                                                            pay our don'ts
spectrum of stoneflies:
glowing in the bark
                of a bleached silk tree
                                        ten times the sun nurses
                        Exceptionalist detriment

Nobody knows our name / S O M E
                                belly back umbilical
                                egg in eye
                                        Exceptional audience
                                        private performance

cavewall   paints dinosexceptionalism
hunt naked   leftovers
                our sun
                        needs our little fingers

                        every river still
                                already
                                blessed blind
including but not
                limited to the sun
                                dead before
                                        excepted
                                skeletons: the earth's nail growth

Expecting   no exception to Exceptionalism

Exceptionalist dawnhoppers: bristleless brooms spreading sun
                                                        skulls

                                killed the everyman

poet's prose

Needs. We need to die. And as Blind Willie Johnson rasped over his guitar, "Dying will be easy." Especially here. In the Big Easy. Or here. In the sea. Or here. Away. In another place. Or certainly here. In space. On land. We are placed on this planet by forces unknown to us. This planet is an easy place to die. Your town too is an easy place to die. The city is an easy place to die. Villages are even easier places to die. The wilderness was once the easiest place to die. We have deaths aplenty. This book is a journey through the bookended history of poetry localized in the most magical place in America. The poems are eager to turn you on to death. Not erotically. Nor religiously. Nor philosophically. Simply. May they ease you as they ease me. We are all death's children and we've yet to stop squirming but poetry is our grandmothers' whiskey dipped pacifier. Poems are also words living on a page. Simple moments when world rings instead of your cell. Lies. Allure. Ignorance, removed. Awake. A wake for experience. Now we live. And I needed to begin where I lived for the first time: New Orleans.

People talk about New York, or even more commonly, California falling into the sea. This talk amuses me with images that I am perversely attracted to—an entire state capsizing like a ship with populations leaping overboard to test their skills at treading water. I've always viewed the sea as the Earth's womb. I find it only fitting that human life gets washed back into the sea at some point. Turns out Louisiana is winning the race. This is the land falling into the sea—the submerged edge of Western Civilization's boot.

Winter after Katrina, I was in Yellowstone with my family visiting the hot springs and read the name for bacteria that thrives in these extreme climates; this bacteria also creates colorful, intricate patterns in the runoff channels. I immediately identified the term with my community. Residents of New Orleans behave and more importantly misbehave as thermophiles. All that has been done to aver New Orleans has been accomplished by its residents. The degrees of dedication are not measured by this writer save one. And this one degree is all any New Orleanian or any lover of any place or person pulled in the rapids of time ever has to fight for: presence.

how's my dying?
please call 202-456-6213[1]

    As the Information Age beaded down the pane into the Dysinformation Age, our high definition screens diluted our quality of death—over-pixelating our connections. When I crafted these poems from line fragments into the book you have before you, I ended up experiencing lives other than my own. The more lives the more deaths and yes disasters die too. But the disasters that we should be held most accountable for are the ones that we repeat—the lives, the ones we refuse to live, and the deaths, the ones we control. We will handle unknown, horrible horizons but the mistakes of yesterday have become the scorpion that strikes its head with its own stinger.

    Katrina stars in *An Easy Place/To Die* and yes she was typecast as the sexy vixen—bringing out the "best and worst of humanity." My muses are New Orleans and the Gulf South, but my admiration extends to the storm because she was the moment when we cried out. I cried out "¡feliz extinction!", which is the book's boldest line. This line compounds in relevance when we replace the star of yesterday with the star of today: the BP Gulf Coast Oil Leak—our new, "latest sapping." "Causeway" is a presence that perseveres collapse and immolation, and as I listen to our nation's cries quelled before they started, and I continue to watch the controlled burns and dispersant contamination, I return to my poem re-informed. This leak is our second sting. Louisiana *is* at the edge of Western Civilization. And as I type this afterword (on the Fourth of July 2010, oil filling the Gulf as fireworks fill the sky) it occurs to me, extinction is no longer an exaggeration.

    For now, this Exceptionalist writer just wants to acknowledge this event as a fact. The leak is listed in "Causeway" (a list I promised I would stop adding years to as soon as the book was published), it's a transition point for contemporary Thermophile consciousness, it's the immediate villain to the coastal Louisiana residents and our environment, and it's also the present plot of our nation. Although New Orleans and the surrounding areas are now popular settings and hosts for the entertainment industry, this disaster is not a movie; we can ride no further west. America, begin again and again with your Thermophiles.

---

[1] The White House's comment line

mise en place

This book applies and embellishes Joyce's organizational scaffolding, used in *Ulysses*, by double retrofitting episodes from *Gilgamesh* and sections from *The Waste Land* (arguably the "first" and "last" poems) to contextualize my work with words in the *nagbu* or well of poetic history. There are numerous resonances in content and form to these works and others (unlike the Modernists, I have few urges to cite them)—none of which is important to enjoy the music, enjambment, language innovation, and projective verse of the poems, which are my priorities.

Gilgamesh lost his best friend Enkidu, the wild beast that conflicted with, yet completed his intellect. He exhausts the Earth journeying to find immortality for his friend but fails. New Orleans is my Enkidu. By extension Enkidu is also a city. Gilgamesh's capital was Uruk, which is where the book begins. The "Uruk—cradlecasket" sequence pairs Eliot's "Burial of the Dead" with mythmaking, poetry of the past, and a life cycle.

The title of the sequence "Ishtar's Castles" is a composite of the fertility goddess and "A Game of Chess." The poems wander through the social world, specifically the defenses and offenses of lovemaking. I replaced some of these love poems' irksome personal pronouns with the neologism nother. It is an endearing kenning for no other. It also amuses me because in full, the word is genderless; but if split apart differently, it reveals two paradoxes. Nother also appears in *Ulysses* as a typo in a telegram which was intended to read: "mother dying."

The penultimate sequence is intensely personal and examines uncontrollable events. The Bull of Heaven is the consequence of Gilgamesh's rejection of the goddess and results in Enkidu's death because he too insults her. This section alludes to "Death by Water" by replacing drought with water imagery, where the self eventually drowns.

In the final sequence, the lyric returns as an elixir to extinction, and the book climatically concludes with a long, projective finale of the work and the city. "Causeway" is the Thermophile version of Crane's *The Bridge* collapsed. A broken eternity sign divides the sections.

The two appendices: a verse "Manifesto" and "Womanifesto" are included as theoretical derivatives from New Orleans, an Exceptional environment. They were the first two things I wrote after this book and they are claims for future verse.

The "Fire Sermon" is intrinsically connected to the Thermophiles in "Causeway." Give, sympathize, and control—the final mandates of "What the Thunder Said"—are updated in the book's first poem to give, empathize, and create.

Thermophiles continue to cultivate our magical plants to revive Enkidu. Some nights we do.

about the poet

Vincent A. Cellucci is a traveling neologist. He received his MFA from Louisiana State University and went to Loyola University New Orleans for his bachelor's degree in writing. He has been published in *Exquisite Corpse*, *moira*, *New Delta Review*, *The Pedestal*, and *Presa*; he contributed, edited, and produced a collaborative audio novel entitled *The Katrina Decameron* (2010); and he teaches communication in LSU's College of Art + Design. In his spare time, he paints and scuba dives.

For additional author information please visit www.vincentacellucci.com.

acknowledgments

I am grateful to the editors of the following literary journals where these poems first appeared: *Big Bridge* ("Cleaning Up/Al's Apartment" and "responsorial"), *Exquisite Corpse* (segments of "Causeway" under the title "Thermophiles", "Exceptionalist Manifesto", and "Exceptionalist Womanifesto"), *The Pedestal* ("Matter/For Mourning"), *New Delta Review* ("Upriver" and "I had a Room in New Orleans"), and *Presa* ("Remnants"). Heartfelt thanks to Peyton Burgess, Colleen H. Fava, Matthew Landers, and my parents, Anthony and Leigh, for helping me read and ready the prose sections of this book. Exceptional thanks to Andrei and Laura Codrescu who stoked Exceptionalism's hibernatationattack in their summer caves and then published the results.

Thanks to all the poets who have helped intensify my verse, especially Eric Elliott, Brock Guthrie, Ben Lowenkron, and Chris Shipman. Debangana Banerjee and Laura Mullen, your constant support aided me more than you know throughout the publication process. I also wish to acknowledge two women scholars that I am privileged to call my personal friends and professional mentors: Dr. Mary McCay and Dr. Lillian Bridwell-Bowles; may you both consider this accomplishment directly due to your positive impacts in my life. Utmost thanks to my editor, Gregg Wilhelm, without whom this book would not be possible; nevermind cool, you are bad ass, and I consider being published by you and CityLit Press as the highest compliment. Jonas Kyle-Sidell deserves praise too for the work he has put into the design and the layout of this book; thank you all.

CityLit Press's mission is to provide a venue for writers who might otherwise be overlooked by larger publishers due to the literary nature or regional focus of their projects. It is the imprint of nonprofit CityLit Project, founded in Baltimore in 2004.

CityLit nurtures the culture of literature in Baltimore and throughout Maryland by creating enthusiasm for literature, building a community of avid readers and writers, and opening opportunities for young people and diverse audiences to embrace the literary arts. Its family of programs instill and sustain a life-long love of literature.

Thank you to our major supporters: the Maryland State Arts Council, the Baltimore Office of Promotion and The Arts, and the Baltimore Community Foundation. CityLit Festival, our signature program, is also supported by the National Endowment for the Arts. More information and documentation is available at www.guidestar.org.

Additional support is provided by individual contributors. Financial support is vital for sustaining the on-going work of the organization. Secure, on-line donations can by made at our web site, click on "Donate."

CityLit is a member of the Greater Baltimore Cultural Alliance, the Maryland Association of Nonprofit Organizations, Maryland Citizens for the Arts, and the Writers' Conferences and Centers division of the Association of Writers and Writing Programs (AWP). In 2010, CityLit established offices in the School of Comunications Design at the University of Baltimore.

For submission guidelines, information about CityLit Press's poetry chapbook contests, and all the programs and services offered by CityLit, please visit www.citylitproject.org.

Nurturing the culture of literature.

www.ingramcontent.com/pod-product-compliance
Lightning Source LLC
Chambersburg PA
CBHW030003050426
42451CB00006B/98